RICKY CLEMONS

PUBLISHED BY FIEDLI PUBLISHING, INC.

Copyright ©2020, Ricky Clemons

ALL RIGHTS RESERVED.

No part of this publication may be reproduced, stored in a retrieval system, or transmitted in any form or by any means—electronic, mechanical, photo-copy, recording, or any other—except for brief quotation in reviews, without the prior permission of the author or publisher.

ISBN: 978-1-948638-11-1

Published by

Fideli Publishing, Inc.
119 W. Morgan St.
Martinsville, IN 46151

www.FideliPublishing.com

Contents

Rainbows Have Beautiful Colors 1

I Hear Your Voice 3

Do Good Things 4

When We Have Hope 5

The Lord is Not Slow 6

Life Will Sometimes Be Hard 7

Prayer 8

Unlocked Faith 9

This Christian Journey is Not Easy 10

Our Shepherd is Jesus Christ 11

We Need Love Every Day 12

You Winked Your Eye 13

If You Are 14

Everybody 15

Better Than You 16

Being Yourself 17

Don't Eat that Forbidden Fruit 18

Everybody in the Church Will Not 19

Catch Up with Us 20

You Will Only Live this Life Once 21

It Will Hurt Your Heart, O Lord 22

We Can Believe the Bible 23

In the Night	24
Will Never Get Bored	25
Even Though Life is Not Easy	26
Is It Possible?	27
God Created Me	28
Help Me to Not Go Back There	29
You Give Me Strength	30
The Greatest Love	31
You are Worth Waiting For	32
A Dictionary Life	33
Pouring Out My Heart	34
True Happiness	35
Forever Gone	36
Giving to Others	37
My Heart	38
A Dead Conscious	39
For the Lord	40
Speak Up	41
You Show Mercy on Me	42
God Doesn't Charge Us	43
Self	44
When the Pain	45
On the Body of Life	46
The Darkness of Sin	47

We Will Always
Need Something 48

You Can't Stop Me..49

Real Life Can Be 50

Will Be So Happy...51

Our Hearts Must Be Right 52

Just Because We Are Living
for the Lord 53

There is Something in Our Faith..54

Everybody Has Feelings 55

There is Power in Jesus' Name...56

Playing Christian 57

I Have Free Will..58

I Trust You, O Lord...59

Laws...60

When You Give People Something Good..............................61

The Blind Side of Our Lives..62

The Road that Leads to the Wind 63

Won't Need..64

Boast About Jesus Christ 65

There's No Telling
How Many Times..66

My Prayers 67

No Matter How 68

Things Can Go Wrong 69

When You Know	70
We Need the Lord's Protection	71
A Dream	72
Jesus Will Bring This World to an End	73
Something Great to Look Forward to	74
We Can Be So Sure	75
God is a Relationship God	76
I Don't Have it in My Heart	77
I Am Nothing Without Jesus Christ	78
To be Saved	79
This Dark and Sinful World	80
Boast About Our Weaknesses	81
In Real Life	82
Where This World is Heading	83
There are All Kinds of Temptations	84
A New World Began	85
In Our Hearts	86
The Lord Predestined Us	87
Being Selfish	88
Just Because We Are Christians	89
O Lord, I Need You so Much	90
In the Bad Weather of Life	91
The Devil's Work	92
After This Life is Over	93

It's Easy to Sin Against God 94

Fighting in a War of Sin 95

Blessed with Enough 96

We Church Folks..97

Your Feelings Can Get Hurt..98

When the Lord Wakes Me Up 99

God Is..100

A Storm Can Frighten Us 101

A Smile Can Lift People Up..102

Mr. Selfishness and Mr. Humility...103

Civilized..104

Speak the Truth in Love 105

Worth Putting Above 106

Miraculous 107

The Power of the Holy Ghost 108

If It Were Possible 109

God's Reasons..110

Being a Christian 111

The Truth..112

There is a True Living God 113

Dealing with Self 114

When the Lord Tells Us 115

Life is Short 116

Just Because You Are 117

Until Our Love is Tested 118
Most of the Time 119
As Light as a Feather 120
Not a Place to Go To...121
There is Not a Day That Goes By 122
There Are People in this World 123
Comfortable...124
We Don't Have to Explain 125
We Don't Have to Explain 126

Rainbows Have Beautiful Colors

Rainbows have beautiful colors, arching over high up in the sky.

Rainbows can appear after the rain, and the sun will shine again near the rainbow.

Inspirational poems are like rainbows that have different colors and look so beautiful.

Each poem about the Lord is like a different color that stands out to read or recite.

Rainbows are always beautiful to look at.

Inspirational poetry, especially in the book of Psalms, are like a beautiful rainbow with different beautiful colors representing different poets.

Every inspirational poem is like a beautiful rainbow that every inspired poet would believe to be a blessing from the Lord.

A rainbow has beautiful colors that God Himself created.

Different rainbow colors have a different meaning, just like every poem has a different meaning.

Every rainbow is a sign of God's promise to the whole world.

It's in the Rainbow

God's promise to us is in the rainbow's sign that this world is not being destroyed by water again.

Regardless of many worldwide water floods, God will keep His promise to us.

O, what a beautiful promise from the rainbow that looks so beautiful up in the sky after the rain.

There are rainbows all around this world. Where God's promise to us is seen.

God could have given us his promise through something else that might not have looked so beautiful.

The rainbows let us know that all of God's promises are beautiful all around this world.

God has made us a promise to destroy this world by fire next time.

That promise is in His holy word that is so beautiful to every Christian who studies and lives by it every day.

The beautiful rainbow is a great thing to look at and not want to ever forget.

God made the beautiful rainbow because He knew that it would get our attention and make us believe His promise during our lifetime on earth.

I Hear Your Voice

I hear Your voice, O Lord, in my mind.

You tell me to love and obey You all the time.

I hear Your voice, O Lord, in my heart.

You tell me that You are always near to me and not far away.

I hear Your voice, O Lord, in my life.

You tell me to live my life unto You, my Lord Jesus Christ.

I hear Your voice, O Lord, throughout the day.

You tell me that You number my days, regardless of what anyone says with their ifs and buts.

I hear Your voice, O Lord, in Your holy word.

You tell me that You so loved me first, even when I didn't love You or truly care to know You.

Do Good Things

Doing good things is not always easy to do.

There are people who will be offended by the good things you and I do.

There are people who don't like for you and me to do good things.

Doing good things can be a wonderful experience and very uplifting.

Doing good things will surely make this world a much better place to live in day after day.

All good things come from the Lord because He is so good to us all the time.

The devil can't do anything good.

He can only pretend to do good things to deceive you and me.

There is no good in the devil, who is all bad every day.

It's always good to tell the truth.

There are people who don't' like to hear the truth that will set them free from lies.

Doing good things has caused many people to lose their lives.

They did not lose their good name; that will live on.

Doing good things in Jesus' name will give the heavens joy.

When We Have Hope

When we have hope, we can hold our heads up.

When we have hope, we have something to look forward to.

When we have hope, we can cheer up.

When we have hope, we can go the extra mile.

When we have hope, we can keep on going.

When we have hope, we have a good thing.

When we have hope, we can smile.

When we have hope, life is worth living.

When we have hope, we have some peace

The greatest hope is putting our hope in Jesus Christ.

Jesus is our only true living hope to hold onto every day.

Jesus is the hope that is eternal beyond this world.

We can't put our hope in this world where hope can fade away.

The Lord is Not Slow

The Lord is not slow to speak to us to do what is right.

We can be slow to listen to the Lord to do what is right

The Lord is not slow to help us.

We can be slow to accept the Lord's help.

The Lord is not slow to supply all of our needs.

We can be slow to not see our needs.

The Lord is not slow to forgive us our sins.

We can be slow to forgive ourselves.

The Lord is not slow to cleanse us of our sins.

We can be slow to confess and repent of our sins.

The Lord is not slow to save us from our sins.

We can be slow to not let go of our sins.

The Lord is not slow to bless us.

We can be slow to not thank the Lord for blessing us.

The Lord is not slow to give us His Holy Spirit.

We can be slow to yield to the Holy Spirit.

Life Will Sometimes Be Hard

Life will sometimes be hard for you and me, who want to love and obey Jesus Christ day after day.

Living in sin is so easy to do because it is easy to do wrong.

Living right by the Lord will be hard sometimes, but it will be very rewarding to our souls.

It can be hard sometimes to speak the truth to people who don't want to hear it.

It is so easy to keep our mouths shut and not speak the truth to people who need to hear it.

It's so easy to do our own will day after day.

Life will sometimes be hard, but doing the Lord's will give us joy and peace that will last our lifetimes.

It's not hard to lean to our own ways and do as we please.

There is no way out for selfish people to not reap what they sow.

It is better to go through some hard times for the Lord than to have it easy while living in sin.

At the end of this world, the wicked who had it easy will surely have it the hardest because they are lost in their sins.

Prayer

When the Lord answers our prayers, it is supernatural.

Prayer is a supernatural thing in our lives.

It is supernatural that prayer makes good things happen to us.

Prayer is extraordinary to change us so we do much better in life.

Prayer makes luck look so worthless.

There is power in prayer that is worthy to make good things happen to us.

The Lord doesn't answer everybody's prayers.

Everybody's prayers are not from the heart.

The Lord will not answer our prayers if we are willfully living in sin and don't want to change and give up our evil ways

Jesus Christ, our Lord and Savior, is forever alive up in heaven to answer our prayers.

Prayer gets our lives moving in the right direction.

Prayer is where Jesus loves for us to confess and repent of our sins.

Unlocked Faith

Unlocked faith is a faith in Jesus that is shared with the world wherever we go here and there.

Unlocked faith is a faith in Jesus to share with others in sermons.

Unlocked faith is a faith in Jesus to share with others in testimonies about Jesus.

Unlocked faith is a faith in Jesus to share with others in our lives that we live unto Jesus.

We must show the world that our faith in Jesus is not locked up in chains of doubt about Him.

We must show the world that our faith in Jesus is not locked up in worries.

We must show the world that Jesus gave us the key to unlock our faith in Him so he can be seen in our lives.

This Christian Journey is Not Easy

On a gospel CD album, you want all the songs to sound perfect.

That may not always get done, especially for the executive producer and producer.

This Christian journey is not easy.

You want your inspirational book to be perfect, without any errors.

That may not always get done, especially for the author.

This Christian journey is not easy.

While being a Sabbath school teacher, you want to teach the truth, but that may not be understood by all in your class.

This Christian journey is not easy.

While being a pastor, you want to preach the truth in love, but some church members may think that you are judging them.

This Christian journey is not easy.

You want to love everybody like a Christian should do, but some people just won't like you because you don't gossip and backbite.

This Christian journey is not easy.

You want to keep your faith in Jesus Christ, but this world will try to seduce your mind with its attractions of material things.

This Christian journey is not easy, but Jesus is worth the journey every day.

Our Shepherd is Jesus Christ

One day in the early morning, a shepherd led his flock of sheep out into the field.

Near the field there is a pond for the sheep to drink from.

The shepherd led his sheep to the pond to drink some water.

One of his sheep drank some water and then took off across the field all alone.

There, across the field, was a wolf that was looking at the lone sheep, thinking he would like to trick it into coming close to him.

The wolf had come up with the idea to camouflage himself so he would look like a sheep.

As the sheep wandered astray in the field, it saw another sheep coming toward him across the field.

The sheep didn't know that the other sheep was a wolf getting ready to eat him up.

During that time, the shepherd called out for his lost sheep, but it didn't hear his voice because it had wandered so far from the flock.

The wolf, still looking like a sheep, saw his plan to deceive the sheep was working as it came close to him.

It was in striking range, and all the wolf had to do was attack the sheep.

All of the sudden, the shepherd came out of nowhere and struck the wolf over the head with his shepherd's crook.

The shepherd had saved his lost sheep from the jaws of the wolf.

Our shepherd is Jesus Christ, who can save us from that old wolf called the devil, who loves to camouflage himself and fool us into thinking he's a good Christian, when he's really there to lead us astray.

We Need Love Every Day

We need love every day that love helps us to survive.

We need love every day that love keeps us going strong.

We need love every day that love is good for us.

We need love every day that love is good for our minds.

We need love every day that love is good for our hearts.

We need love every day that God loves to give to us.

We need love every day that we can't live without.

We need love every day that Jesus Christ is the love of God.

We need love every day that we need to love Jesus Christ.

We need love every day that we need to love one another.

We need love every day that love is God.

We need love every day that love makes no one ill.

We need love every day that love heals broken hearts.

We need love every day that love is stronger than death.

You Winked Your Eye

O Lord, You winked Your eye at my ignorance when I had no knowledge of Your holy word.

O Lord, You winked Your eye at my ignorance when I didn't know a lot of right from wrong.

O Lord, You winked Your eye at my ignorance when I was living in the darkness of my sins.

O Lord, You winked Your eye at my ignorance when I made a lot of bad choices.

O Lord, You winked Your eye at my ignorance when I still had to suffer for living in my sins.

O Lord, You winked Your eye at my ignorance when I still had to suffer for making bad choices.

O Lord, You winked Your eye at my ignorance when I still had to suffer for not yielding to Your Holy Spirit.

O Lord, You winked Your eye at my ignorance and gave me a second chance to not die in my sins.

If You Are

If you are smart, it doesn't mean that you won't make a mistake.

If you are good, it doesn't mean that you will live a very long life.

If you are bad, it doesn't mean that you will live a very short life.

If you are right, it doesn't mean that you will win an argument.

If you are wrong, it doesn't mean that you will feel bad.

If you are beautiful, it doesn't mean that you are in good health.

If you are small, it doesn't mean that you are in bad health.

If you are short, it doesn't mean that you can't do something great.

If you are tall, it doesn't mean that you will be successful in life.

If you are a genius, it doesn't mean that you can't' do something foolish.

If you are Christian, it doesn't mean that you can't commit a sin.

Everybody

You can't talk to everybody, but you can be nice to everybody.

You can't talk to everybody, but you can pray for everybody.

You can't talk to everybody, but you can love everybody.

You can't talk to everybody, but you can respect everybody.

You can't help everybody, but you can be nice to everybody.

You can't help everybody, but you can pray for everybody.

You can't help everybody, but you can love everybody.

You can't understand everybody, but you can be nice to everybody.

You can't understand everybody, but you can pray for everybody.

You can't understand everybody, but you can love everybody.

You can't understand everybody, but you can respect everybody.

You can't relate to everybody, but you can be nice to everybody.

You can't relate to everybody, but you can love everybody.

You can't relate to everybody, but you can respect everybody.

Everybody can be saved from their sins if we confess and repent and believe in Jesus Christ.

Better Than You

Only the Lord knows you better than you.
No human being knows you better than you.
You pretty much know what you can do.
You pretty much know what you can't do.
You pretty much know what you are good at doing.
Only the Lord knows you better than you.
You pretty much know how much you can take.
You pretty much know your weaknesses.
No human being knows your heart better than you.
No human being knows your mind better than you.
No human being knows your choices better than you.
No human being knows what you will say better than you.
Only the Lord knows you better than you.

Being Yourself

Does being yourself mean that you can say anything you want to say?

Many people will be themselves and say bad, negative words that hurt people's reputations.

Does being yourself mean that you can do anything you want to do?

Many people will be themselves and do bad things and not even care what they're doing.

Being about the Lord Jesus Christ is so much better than being yourself.

We must deny self to pick up our cross and follow Jesus Christ.

Being yourself is not denying yourself to follow Jesus Christ, who is forevermore greater than self.

Does being yourself mean that you can't get you into trouble.

Does being yourself mean that you can't ruin you.

Being like Jesus will never get you into trouble.

Being like Jesus will never ruin you.

Does being yourself mean that you can't shorten your life.

Does being yourself mean that you can deceive you.

Being yourself is only a good thing if you surrender your will unto the Lord.

You can't put your trust in being yourself.

You and I can put our trust in Jesus Christ, who knows us better than we know ourselves.

Don't Eat that Forbidden Fruit

Don't eat the forbidden fruit of lust.

Don't eat the forbidden fruit of prejudice.

Don't eat the forbidden fruit of injustice.

Don't eat the forbidden fruit of fornication.

Don't eat the forbidden fruit of adultery.

Don't eat the forbidden fruit of unnatural affection.

Don't eat the forbidden fruit of greed.

Don't eat the forbidden fruit of pride.

Don't eat the forbidden fruit of killing.

Don't eat the forbidden fruit of gossip.

Don't eat the forbidden fruit of selfishness.

Don't eat the forbidden fruit of discontentment.

Eve and Adam ate that forbidden fruit of discontent and disobedience.

Eve wasn't content to live with the way that God created her.

Adam wasn't content to live without Eve after she ate the forbidden fruit.

Lucifer wasn't content with only being an angel.

He wanted to be God.

Everybody in the Church Will Not

Everybody in the church will not give Jesus the glory and praise when prosperity comes their way.

Everybody in the church will not hold onto Jesus when trials come their way.

Everybody in the church will not pray to Jesus when temptations come their way.

Everybody in the church will not call on the name of Jesus when fear comes their way.

Everybody in the church will not trust Jesus when their enemies come their way.

Everybody in the church will not love Jesus when death comes their way.

Everybody in the church will not listen to Jesus when the devil comes their way.

Everybody in the church will not uplift Jesus when trouble comes their way.

Catch Up with Us

When our bad eating habits catch up with us, it can hurt our health.

When our bad drinking habits catch up with us, it can hurt our health.

The bad things we do will catch up with us, and can shorten our lives.

The bad words we say will catch up with us, and hurt our reputations.

The good things we will do will catch up with us, and can prolong our lives.

The good words we say will catch up with us, and bless our lives.

We will reap what we sow, and it will catch up with us and show and tell in our lives.

Living a Christian life will catch up with us, and we will be saved in Jesus Christ.

Living a sinful life will catch up with us, and we will be lost in our sins.

Living a Christian life will catch up with us, and we will go to heaven one day.

Living a sinful life will catch up with us, and we will go to hell one day.

Loving Jesus Christ will catch up with us, and we will keep His commandments.

You Will Only Live this Life Once

Love people while you can.
Treat people right while you can.
You will only live this life once.

Help people while you can.
Encourage people while you can.
You will only live this life once.

Be good to people while you can.
Bless people while you can.
You will only live this life once.

Talk to people about the Lord while you can.
Pray for people while you can.
You will only live this life once.

Live right by example while you can.
Treat people fair while you can.
You will only live this life once.

Save people's lives while you can.
Forgive people while you can.
Tell people the truth while you can.
You will only live this life once.

It Will Hurt Your Heart, O Lord

It will hurt Your heart, O Lord, for You to destroy the fallen angels in hell.

It will hurt Your heart, O Lord, for You to destroy lost souls in hell.

O Lord, You love all the angels You created.

O Lord, You love every human being You created.

O Lord, You would never have created the angels if You didn't' love them.

O Lord, You would have never created human beings if You didn't love them.

O Lord, You love all creatures that You created for Your enjoyment.

It will hurt Your heart, O Lord, to destroy what You created.

No angel and no human being can ever know how much it will hurt Your heart, O Lord, for You to one day burn up fallen angles and lost souls in hell.

We Can Believe the Bible

The things that are going on in this world are evidence of what the bible says.

Many people believe lies to be the truth.

We can never be wrong for believing the truth in the bible.

The bible tells us the truth about God, when many people believe there is no God.

The bible tells us the truth about people.

The bible tells us about the wicked man and the righteous man.

The ways of the wicked man are evidence of what the bible says.

The ways of the righteous man are also evidence of what the bible says.

We can always believe the bible.

God is evidence of what the bible says.

We can know God in the bible, where God talks to us with love.

In the Night

Unfaithful people will cheat on their girlfriend, boyfriend, spouse pretty much in the night.

Stealing will go on pretty much in the night.

Prostitution will happen pretty much in the night.

Parties will go on pretty much in the night.

Drunk people are drunk pretty much in the night.

Entertaining people will go on pretty much in the night.

People will sleep pretty much in the night.

Most dreams are in the night.

Most stars are seen in the night.

Most romance happens in the night.

Most murders are in the night.

People will get lost pretty much in the night.

Most crimes are in the night.

We are living in the night of this world.

Jesus Christ is coming back again like a thief in the night.

Will Never Get Bored

The sun will never get bored with shining all day long.

The moon will never get bored with glowing all night long.

The stars will never get bored with sparkling all night long.

The sky will never get bored with hovering over the earth.

The rain will never get bored with falling from the sky.

The trees will never get bored with standing up tall.

The grass will never get bored with covering the ground.

You and I can get bored if we have nothing to say.

The ground will never get bored with holding this world together.

The leaves will never get bored with falling off trees.

Our hearts will never get bored with what we feel.

Our minds will never get bored with what we think.

Jesus Christ will never get bored with cleansing us of our sins.

Jesus Christ will never get bored with saving us from our sins.

Jesus Christ will never get bored with loving us.

Jesus Christ will never get bored with answering our prayers.

Jesus Christ will never get bored with forgiving us of our sins.

Even Though Life is Not Easy

Even though life is not easy, my Lord and Savior Jesus Christ opens doors for you and me.

Even though life is not easy, my Lord and Savior Jesus Christ will make a way out of no way for you and me.

Even though life is not easy, my Lord and Savior Jesus Christ will answer our prayers according to His holy will.

Even though life is not easy, my Lord and Savior Jesus Christ will bless you and me.

Even though life is not easy, my Lord and Savior Jesus Christ will supply all of our needs.

Even though life is not easy, my Lord and Savior Jesus Christ will protect you and me.

Even though life is not easy, my Lord and Savior Jesus Christ will never leave us or forsake us.

Even though life is not easy, my Lord and Savior Jesus Christ can prolong our lives so we can live a long time.

Is It Possible?

Is it possible that there were some women and children who wanted to get on Noah's ark and were held captive against their will to stop them from getting on the ark?

If that is true, will they be saved when Jesus Christ comes back again?

Is it possible that the people who were resurrected from the grave when Jesus was resurrected went back to heaven with Jesus?

There were many people who walked through the Jerusalem city and people were eyewitnesses to this.

Is it possible that some of the Pharisees, Sadducees and some of the Roman soldiers believed in Jesus Christ before they died?

Is it possible that Adam and Eve shed many tears after they sinned against God, who put them out of the Garden of Eden?

They knew that their lives would never be perfect again.

Is it possible that Jesus Christ will come back again in our lifetime?

Are we ready to see Him on the clouds of glory?

Are we ready to go back to heaven with Jesus?

God Created Me

God created me to be of average intelligence.

I like the way God created me.

God created many people to be geniuses.

God created many people to be highly intelligent.

God created many people to be intellectuals.

Don't look down on me for being of average intelligence.

That is the way God made me.

I am content with that.

I like the way God created me.

God knows what is good for me.

Always like the way God created you.

If you are brilliant or highly intelligent, you can give God the glory and praise.

There are things that God put into our genes.

If average intelligence is in your genes — God put it there.

If genius is in your genes — God put that there, too.

If brilliance is in your genes — God put it there.

God doesn't make mistakes in the way He creates us, even if we feel like we are a mistake.

God knows that everybody can't handle being a genius, brilliant or highly intelligent.

Help Me to Not Go Back There

O Lord, help me to not go back there and hold grudges against the people who hurt my heart.

O Lord, help me to not go back there and talk bad about the people who used me.

O Lord, help me to not go back there and get revenge against the people who did me wrong.

O Lord, help me to not go back there and talk bad to the people who talked bad to me.

O Lord, help me to not go back there to the bad things that happened to me.

I can truly thank You for not letting the bad things kill me.

My Lord and Savior Jesus Christ, You didn't go back there to get revenge at the Pharisees for telling lies about You.

My Lord and Savior Jesus Christ, You didn't go back there to kill the Roman soldiers who nailed You on the cross.

O Lord, help me to be more forgiving, like You.

You Give Me Strength

O Lord, You give me strength in my mind to help keep my thoughts in line with Your holy word that is good for me all the time.

O Lord, You give me strength in my heart to keep my feelings in line with Your holy word that is deep, eternal truth for me who is a chief among sinners.

O Lord, You give me strength in my body to be Your holy temple according to Your holy word.

I seek to do right for Your service, O Lord.

O Lord, You give me strength in my life so I can live my life according to Your holy word that shows me Your will that will always bless my life.

The Greatest Love

The greatest love is to love Jesus Christ.

If you love yourself more than you love Jesus, you will fail yourself.

Jesus will never fail you if you love Him more than you love yourself.

The greatest love is to love Jesus Christ.

If you love anyone else more than you love Jesus, you will get deceived.

Jesus will never deceive you for loving him more than anyone else.

The greatest love is to love Jesus Christ.

If you love anything more than you love Jesus, you will ruin yourself.

Jesus will never ruin you if you love Him more than anything in this world.

The greatest love is to love Jesus Christ.

If you love your life more than you love Jesus, you will cheat your life.

Jesus will never cheat your life if you love Him more than you love your own life.

The greatest love is to love Jesus Christ.

If you love this world more than you love Jesus Christ, you will just fool yourself.

Jesus will never fool you if you love Him more than loving this world.

The greatest love is to love Jesus Christ.

You are Worth Waiting For

O Lord, You are worth waiting for, even if it takes years for You to give me victory over the bad things in my life.

O Lord, I want to wait for You because I am tired of doing things I regret because I did them my own way.

O Lord, I need to wait for You, because I am tired of messing things up in my life.

O Lord, You are worth waiting on because You give me peace.

O Lord, I have taken some things in my own hands and I am surely paying for it the hard way now.

O Lord, You let me know that waiting for You is the right thing to do every day.

O Lord, I want to wait for You because life is too short to keep making the same mistakes over and over again.

Waiting for You, my Lord and Savior Jesus Christ, will keep me from making the same mistakes over and over again.

O Lord, You are always worth waiting for, because You can surely work things out for me no matter what.

I have done some things without waiting for You, O Lord, and it caught up with me and I regret it.

You are worth waiting for, O Lord, and I thank You for helping me to see the light.

A Dictionary Life

We are people who live a dictionary life.

There are definitions for everyone and everything.

There are people who have a definition for what people say.

There are people who have a definition for the way people dress.

There are people who have a definition for whatever people do.

There are people who have a definition for the way people look.

There are people who have a definition for people's motives.

There are people who have a definition for people's intentions.

There are people who live a dictionary life.

They believe that they must always be right about what they define to be true.

Back in the bible days, the Pharisees lived a dictionary life, too.

They always defined Jesus Christ as a threat to them.

Even Jesus' very own close neighbors defined Jesus as "only a carpenter."

Pouring Out My Heart

Pouring Out my heart unto You, my Lord, will strengthen my faith in You.

Pouring Out my heart unto You, my Lord, will bring tears to my eyes.

Pouring Out my heart unto You, my Lord, will draw me closer to You.

Pouring Out my heart unto You, my Lord, will open my eyes to see more of Your truth.

Pouring Out my heart unto You, my Lord, is a wonderful experience.

Pouring Out my heart unto You, my Lord, will humble me more and more.

Pouring Out my heart unto You, my Lord, lifts me up and helps me to keep my eyes on You.

Pouring Out my heart unto You, my Lord, helps me to love and obey You.

True Happiness

Having faith in You, O Lord, gives me true happiness.

Trusting You, O Lord, gives me true happiness.

Loving You, O Lord, gives me true happiness.

Holding onto You, O Lord, gives me true happiness.

Praying to You, O Lord, gives me true happiness.

Material things can't give me true happiness.

This world can't give me true happiness.

Only You, My Lord and Savior Jesus Christ, can give me true happiness.

Being saved in You, O Lord, gives me true happiness.

Keeping my mind on You, O Lord, gives me true happiness.

Being strong in You, O Lord, gives me true happiness.

Having a relationship with You, O Lord, gives me true happiness.

Putting my hopes in You, O Lord, gives me true happiness.

Forever Gone

When a bubble bursts, it's forever gone.

When a raindrop falls on the ground, it's forever gone.

When we swallow food down to our bellies, it's forever gone.

When we wake up out of a dream, it's forever gone.

When someone dies, he or she is forever gone.

When water runs down a drain, it's forever gone.

When a thought is not remembered, it's forever gone.

When a snowflake melts, it's forever gone.

When Jesus forgives us of our sins, it's forever gone.

When Jesus cleanses us of our sins, it's forever gone.

When Jesus saves us from our sins, it's forever gone.

When Jesus burns up the wicked, they will be forever gone.

Giving to Others

Giving to others is a very uplifting experience.

It helps to keep you and me from only thinking about ourselves.

When you and I give good things to others, it will brighten up our lives with joy.

Giving to others can surely cheer people up if they receive what you give to them and you ask nothing in return.

Giving to others is always a good thing to do.

It helps you and me get rid of our attachment to ourselves.

Jesus Christ, our Lord and Savior, was a very giving man, giving to all who would receive his blessings when he lived on earth.

Jesus was the most selfless man when he lived on earth without sin.

Jesus always gave good things to others, and he did it with a pure heart.

We live in a world today where many people believe you and I want something in return if we give them something good for free.

They may also believe that we are weird for doing this.

The more you and I give to others, the more selfless we will become.

We can never give enough for Jesus.

My Heart

My heart is what I do from day to day.

My heart will reveal who I am from day to day.

My heart is a book of motives.

My heart is a battlefield for good against evil.

My heart is a river of feelings.

My heart is a pathway to selfishness.

My heart is a wilderness.

My heart is a hope of morality in Jesus Christ.

My heart is a mountain of love in Jesus Christ.

My heart is a wide-open sky of peace in Jesus Christ.

My heart is an outer space of joy in Jesus Christ.

My heart is an obedience of sunshine in Jesus Christ.

My heart is a treasure of selflessness in Jesus Christ.

A Dead Conscious

Many people in this world have a dead conscious.

They will say something wrong and not feel guilty about it.

They will do something bad and not feel guilty about that either.

Many people in this world have a dead conscious.

They will kill someone and not feel guilty about it.

They will steal and not feel guilty.

They will tell a lie and not feel guilty.

Many people in this world have a dead conscious.

They will disobey their parents and not feel guilty.

They will want what belongs to someone else and not feel guilty about it.

They will get revenge and not feel guilty.

Many people in this world have a dead conscious.

The Holy Spirit can surely make anyone's conscious come alive.

God's holy word is filled with the Holy Spirit, and its truth makes anyone's conscious come alive.

Believing in Jesus Christ will make anyone's conscious come alive and stay alive.

For the Lord

If you're doing something good for the Lord, all of your kinfolks will not be happy for you.

If you're doing something good for the Lord, everybody in the church will not be happy for you.

It makes the devil mad if you are doing something good for the Lord.

Some people will get jealous, if you're doing something good for the Lord.

Some people won't like you, if you're doing something good for the Lord.

Some people will talk bad about you, if you're doing something good for the Lord.

If you are doing something good for the Lord with pure motives, the Lord will continue to bless your ministry.

Doing something good for the Lord will lift you up to spiritual heights in the Lord Jesus Christ.

Speak Up

Sometimes we have to speak up to get something done that we need to get done.

Sometimes we have to speak up and not sit back and say nothing.

Speaking up can get some things done.

Some people will sit back and say nothing while they need something to be done.

Speaking up can save us from some problems.

Speaking up can get things done much faster.

Speaking up can ease our minds.

Speaking up can make us feel much better.

If we sit back and say nothing when we need to say something, we may very well regret it in the long run.

We need to always speak up and ask Jesus for the things we need.

Jesus says that we don't have because we don't ask.

Speaking up surely can do us a lot of good.

You Show Mercy on Me

I don't deserve to have any good things from You, O Lord.

You show mercy on me and give me good things.

I deserve to die in my sins.

You show mercy on me, O Lord, and forgive me of my sins.

I don't deserve to be alive.

You show mercy on me, my Lord Jesus Christ, and let me live another day.

I don't deserve any of Your blessings.

You show mercy on me, my Lord, and bless me.

I don't deserve Your love, my Lord.

You show mercy on me and give me Your everlasting love.

I don't deserve to talk to You, my Lord.

You show mercy on me and listen to what I say to You.

I don't deserve to ask You for anything, O Lord.

You show mercy on me and answer my prayers.

I don't deserve to have a relationship with You, my Lord.

You show mercy on me and have a relationship with me.

I don't deserve to call on Your holy name, my Lord Jesus Christ.

You show mercy on me and give me power and the victory in Your name.

God Doesn't Charge Us

God doesn't charge us to live.

God gives life to us for free.

God doesn't charge us to see.

God gives us eyes for free.

God doesn't charge us to hear.

God gives us ears for free.

God doesn't charge us for physical strength.

God gives us physical strength for free.

God doesn't charge us for the body he gave to us for free.

Many people have a business.

They will charge you and me for their products with an unfair price.

God's Son, Jesus Christ, doesn't charge us to cleanse our sins.

God's Son, Jesus Christ, doesn't charge us to save us from our sins.

If God charged us to be blessed by Him, we wouldn't be able to pay Him for our life, health and strength.

Self

Self is a mountain to climb up to the top.

Self is a valley to walk down into.

Self is an ocean to explore its depths.

Self is the green grass that can turn brown.

Self is a fruit tree that can have some rotten fruit.

Self is the moon that can glow mysteriously.

Self is a storm that can rage.

Self is a ship that can wreck.

Self is a river that can flood the dry land.

Self is a well that can run dry.

Self is a book that can be read.

Self is a jar that can break.

Self is a light bulb that can blow out.

Self is a mattress that can get lumpy.

Self is a door that can be unlocked.

Self is nothing good without Jesus Christ.

When the Pain

When the pain pours down heavy like the rain, pray to Jesus, who can cause the pain to be much lighter.

When the pain feels like it's insane, pray to Jesus, who can cause the pain to be sane.

Heartache is a heavy pain, but Jesus can make it light on you and me.

Jesus is always on time to ease our pain.

We must trust Him to ease our pain, no matter who we are.

Pain is only for a moment, and it strengthens you and me in the Lord Jesus Christ, who we will one day see on the clouds of glory because we are saved.

When the pain burns like red-hot flames, pray to Jesus Christ, who is living water to quench our pain and bless our lives.

On the Body of Life

Death is only a small mole on the body of life.

Life is everywhere around the world.

Death is only a small sore on the body of life.

Life will birth more and more babies around the world.

Death is only a small scratch on the body of life.

Life is from one generation to the next generation.

Death is only a pimple on the body of life.

Life has no end in heaven above this world.

Death is only a freckle on the body of life.

Life is eternal in Jesus Christ.

Death is only a little dry skin on the body of life.

Life is in other worlds so far away from this world.

Death is only a small scar on the body of life.

Jesus Christ will come back again one day and give life a new body with no spots, blemishes or worries of death.

The Darkness of Sin

The darkness of sin is like walking in the dark forest at night.

We don't know what will attack us there.

The darkness of sin is like walking into a dark cave.

We don't know what will attack us there.

The darkness of sin is like walking into a dark tunnel.

We don't know what will attack us there.

The darkness of sin is like walking into a dark old house.

We don't know what will attack us there.

The darkness of sin is like swimming in a river at night.

We don't know what will attack us there.

The darkness of sin is like being lost in a big city at night.

We don't know what will attack us there.

The darkness of sin is like driving a car with no lights at night.

We don't know what we will hit.

Sin is darkness all the time.

There is no light living in sin.

Only Jesus Christ is the light of this world.

Only Jesus Christ can always shine through the darkness of sin.

We Will Always Need Something

In this life, we will always need something day after day.

We need clean water to drink day after day.

We need healthy food to eat day after day.

We need to have good hygiene day after day.

We need a good night's sleep night after night.

We need to exercise day after day.

In this life, we will always need something day after day.

We need money to buy what we need.

We need some good friends to talk to.

We need to love one another day after day.

We need love Jesus Christ day after day.

We need obey Jesus Christ day after day.

We need to read the bible day after day.

We need to live right by the bible day after day.

We need to be saved in Jesus day after day.

We need to give Jesus the glory and praise day after day.

You Can't Stop Me

You may talk bad about me, but you can't stop me from saying good things about my Lord and Savior Jesus Christ.

You may not believe me, but you can't stop me from believing in my Lord and Savior Jesus Christ.

You may not love me, but you can't stop me from loving in my Lord and Savior Jesus Christ.

You may not trust me, but you can't stop me from trusting in my Lord and Savior Jesus Christ.

You may look down on me, but you can't stop me from looking up to my Lord and Savior Jesus Christ.

You may treat me bad, but you can't stop me from obeying my Lord and Savior Jesus Christ.

You may hate me, but you can't stop me from living my life unto my Lord and Savior Jesus Christ.

You may kill me, but you can't stop me from receiving eternal life in my Lord and Savior Jesus Christ.

Real Life Can Be

Real life can be difficult sometimes.

Real life can be complicated sometimes.

Real life can be discouraging sometimes.

Real life can be questioned sometimes.

Real life can be surprising sometimes.

Real life can be good sometimes.

Real life can be wonderful sometimes.

Real life can be rewarding sometimes.

Real life can be a challenge sometimes.

Real life can be simple sometimes.

Real life can be unpredictable sometimes.

Real life can be stressful sometimes.

Real life can be unstable sometimes.

Real life can be disappointing all the time without Jesus Christ.

Will Be So Happy

We will be so happy to see Jesus when He comes back again.

Nothing this world will make us happier than seeing Jesus Christ on the clouds of glory.

We don't know what happiness is until we can be with Jesus forever and ever when he comes back to take you and me to heaven with Him and all the angels.

Jesus will be so happy to see you and me going back to heaven with Him for a thousand years.

We can be so happy to see a loved one who we haven't seen for a long time.

That is nothing compared to seeing Jesus, who we believe in and pray to each and every day.

Every true child of God will be so very happy to see Jesus on the clouds of glory one day.

Our Hearts Must Be Right

When we pray to the Lord for ourselves, our hearts much be right with Him before He will answer our prayers.

When we pray to the Lord for one another, our hearts must be right with everybody for the Lord to answer our prayers.

For our hearts to be right, we must love the Lord.

For our hearts to be right, we must love everybody.

For our hearts to be right, we must love our enemies.

If our hearts are not right with the Lord, then sooner or later it will show and tell in some kind of way.

When we worship the Lord, our hearts must be right.

Just Because We Are Living for the Lord

Just because we are living for the Lord doesn't mean that we won't have heartaches.

Just because we are living for the Lord doesn't mean that we won't have disappointments.

Just because we are living for the Lord doesn't mean that we won't get sick.

Just because we are living for the Lord doesn't mean that we won't have any bad days.

Just because we are living for the Lord doesn't mean that we won't have any problems.

Just because we are living for the Lord doesn't mean that we won't make mistakes.

Just because we are living for the Lord doesn't mean that we will live a long life.

Just because we are living for the Lord doesn't mean that we will always live a good life.

There is Something in Our Faith

There is something in our faith that means we believe in Jesus Christ, who is the Son of God.

There is something in our faith that means we believe in Jesus Christ, who walked on the water and calmed the storm.

There is something in our faith that means we believe in Jesus Christ, who healed the sick and made the lame walk again.

There is something in our faith that means we believe in Jesus Christ, who fed the hungry.

There is something in our faith that means we believe in Jesus Christ, who raised the dead.

There is something in our faith that means we believe in Jesus Christ, who was without sin and died for our sins.

There is something in our faith that means we believe in Jesus Christ, who rose from the grave.

There is something in our faith that means we believe in Jesus Christ, who can cleanse us of our sins and save us from our sins.

Everybody Has Feelings

Everybody can't see.

There are many blind people.

Everybody can't hear.

There are many deaf people.

Everybody can't talk.

There are many mute people

Everybody can't walk.

There are many paralyzed people

Everybody has feelings

Everybody feels something.

Everybody can't talk.

Everybody can feel happy.

Everybody can feel sad.

Everybody can feel good.

Everybody can feel bad.

Everybody can feel bold about doing something.

Everybody can feel afraid about doing something.

Everybody can feel sick.

Everybody can feel angry.

Everybody can feel tired.

When Jesus lived on earth, he had feelings too.

Jesus Christ, our Lord and Savior, feels our joy.

Jesus Christ, our Lord and Savior, feels our sorrows.

There is Power in Jesus' Name

Some years ago, I was a security officer securing some stores, trucking companies, construction sites and some military ships.

One night on my midnight shift, I was securing a military ship and there was another ship in the next dock. As I looked at the ship in the next dock, I felt something supernatural from that ship.

All night long, I felt a supernatural power coming from that ship in the next dock.

When daybreak finally came around, I saw the name of Jesus written on the ship in big black letters.

The big ship was old and looked like it had been all use up. The name of Jesus on that ship was so powerful, I felt it all night long. There is power in Jesus' name, all day long and all night long.

Just by looking at that big ship, the Lord had inspired me to write some inspirational poems.

One of my poems was produced as a gospel song called, "The Admiral of Our Heavenly Ship."

Playing Christian

A lot of people are playing Christian.

They go to church, while living in sin.

A lot of people are playing Christian.

They hold office positions in the church with their pride on display like a rainbow in the sky.

A lot of people are playing Christian.

They have spiritual gifts in the church with no relationship with the Lord Jesus Christ.

A lot of people are playing Christian.

They sing spiritual hymns in the church about the Lord Jesus Christ, while they don't love everybody like Jesus loves everybody.

A lot of people are playing Christian.

They preach, teach and pray before the church congregation, while they are self-righteous and act like they have no sins to confess and repent of.

I Have Free Will

I am not going to let anyone cause me to lose out on my soul salvation because I have free will.

I have free will to choose to say what I want to say.

I have free will to do what I want to do.

Every day, I choose to do the Lord's will.

There is salvation in my Lord and Savior Jesus Christ.

There is no salvation in doing my own will.

I choose not to let anyone cause me to be lost.

My Lord gives me free will that no one can take away from me.

The devil can't take away my free will.

As much as I love my loved ones, I love my free will much more.

I choose Jesus over my loved ones.

Life is too short for me to use my free will to break God's commandments.

God's holy law is freedom that my free will can marvel at.

I Trust You, O Lord

I trust You, O Lord, that You will supply all of my needs.

I trust You, O Lord, that You will work things out for me.

I trust You, O Lord, that You will make a way out of no way for me.

I trust You, O Lord, that You will hear my prayers.

I trust You, O Lord, that You will answer my prayers.

I trust You, O Lord, that You will never forsake me.

I trust You, O Lord, that You will protect me.

I trust You, O Lord, that You will help me.

I trust You, O Lord, that You will never do me wrong.

I trust You, O Lord, that You will lighten my burdens.

I trust You, O Lord, that You will never lie to me.

I trust You, O Lord, that You will not put on me more than what I can bear.

I trust You, O Lord, that only You can save me from my sins.

I trust You, O Lord, that You will always love me.

I trust You, O Lord, that only You can give me eternal life.

Laws

Man's laws can sometimes be crooked.

Man's laws can sometimes be bad.

Man's laws can sometimes be unfair.

Man's laws can sometimes stress people out.

Man's laws can sometimes disappoint people.

Man's laws can sometimes harm people.

Man's laws can sometimes oppress people.

Man's laws can sometimes discourage people.

Man's laws can sometimes anger people.

Man's laws can sometimes divide people.

Man's laws can sometimes make people ill.

God's laws are never crooked.

God's laws are holy.

God's laws are never unfair.

God's laws are righteous.

God's laws are never stressful.

God's laws are healthy.

God's laws are never oppressive.

God's laws are freedom.

God's laws are not temporary.

God's laws are eternal.

Man's laws can sometimes be sinful.

God's laws are always perfect.

When You Give People Something Good

When you give people something good to hold onto, it can last a lot longer than money.

When you give people something good to hold onto, it can surely lift them up if they are feeling down.

When you give people something good to hold onto, it can surely cause them to share it with others.

When you give people something good to hold onto, it can surely make them happy.

When the Lord gives you and me something good, we're supposed to bless others with it.

All good things come from the Lord, who is so good to us all the time.

When you and I give people something good to hold onto, it can surely make us feel so good in our hearts.

The Blind Side of Our Lives

Jesus will always see the blind side of our lives.

You and I can't see the blind side of our lives.

We can't see what is coming up beside us as we drive on the highway of life.

We are blind to not see what a day will bring to us.

We are blind to not see what can happen to us.

We are blind to not see danger coming our way.

Jesus will always see the blind side of our lives.

We must always stay in prayer unto Jesus Christ to protect us from the blind side of our lives.

The blind side of our lives can catch us off guard if we don't choose to do right by the Lord.

The Lord Jesus Christ can surely spare our lives from the harm and danger of the blind side.

Many people will not be cautious about the blind side of their lives.

Many people will overlook the blind side of their lives.

The blind side is never a good thing for anyone to be up against.

The blind side of our lives can wreck our lives if we don't' keep our eyes on Jesus, who will always see and protect us from the blind side of our lives if we obey Him.

The Road that Leads to the Wind

The road that leads to the wind is not living our life unto the holy will of Jesus Christ.

We know that the wind has nothing in it.

Our lives are nothing if we don't love and obey Jesus Christ.

The road that leads to the wind is doing our own will that can blow in different directions without Jesus Christ in our lives.

We can't see the wind and don't know how long it will blow.

We don't know how long we will live; only the Lord knows that.

Just like the Lord knows the road that leads to the wind.

We can't drive on the wind, we can't walk on the wind and we can't hold onto the wind.

We can't depend on the wind to take us to where we want to go.

We can always depend on Jesus Christ, who created the wind to blow.

He is visible in every Christian life in this world, where the wind is invisible and has no substance.

The road that leads to the wind is a road that many people are walking on because they are not saved in Jesus Christ. He is visible in the bible in this world, where the wind is invisible and has no substance.

Won't Need

When we get to heaven we won't need baths and showers.

We will have perfect hygiene forever and ever.

When we get to heaven, we won't need sleep and we will never get tired.

Even the animals won't need sleep and they will never get tired.

When we get to heaven, we won't need coats and hats.

It won't get cold or hot in heaven.

When we get to heaven, we don't need graveyards.

We will live in heaven forever and ever.

When we get to heaven we won't need military forces.

We won't have wars in heaven forever and ever.

When we get to heaven, we won't' need money to buy anything or to pay bills.

Everything in heaven will be free through our Lord and Savior Jesus Christ.

Boast About Jesus Christ

Don't boast about a human being who can lie to you.

Boast about Jesus Christ who will never lie to you.

Don't boast about a human being who can deceive you.

Boast about Jesus Christ who will never deceive you.

Don't boast about a human being who can fail you.

Boast about Jesus Christ who will never fail you.

Don't boast about a human being who can make a mistake.

Boast about Jesus Christ who will never make a mistake.

Don't boast about a human being who has sins to confess and repent.

Boast about Jesus Christ who has no sins.

Don't boast about a human being who can die.

Boast about Jesus Christ who is alive forever and ever.

Don't boast about a human being who can stop loving you.

Boast about Jesus Christ who will never stop loving you.

Don't boast about a human being who can turn against you.

Boast about Jesus Christ who is always there for you to be saved in Him.

There's No Telling How Many Times

There's no telling how many times that You, My Lord, protected me from harm.

There's no telling how many times that You, My Lord, protected me from danger.

There's no telling how many times that You, My Lord, protected me from getting in an accident.

There's no telling how many times that You, My Lord, protected me from looking bad

There's no telling how many times that You, My Lord, protected me from evil.

There's no telling how many times that You, My Lord, protected me from death.

There's no telling how many times that You, My Lord, protected me from saying something I would regret.

There's no telling how many times that You, My Lord, protected me from my enemies.

There's no telling how many times that You, My Lord, protected me from the unknown.

My Prayers

It's beyond the ordinary that You, my Lord, answer my prayers.

It's so great that You, my Lord, answer my prayers.

It's so good that You, my Lord, answer my prayers.

It's so out of this world that You, my Lord, answer my prayers.

It's a miracle that You, my Lord, answer my prayers.

O Lord, You will answer all of Your children's prayers.

O Lord, You will answer my prayers according to Your will.

O Lord, You will answer all of Your children's prayers according to Your will.

O Lord, Your answer may not always be what I expect it to be.

O Lord, Your answers are always for my good.

O Lord, some of Your answers may not always be what I expect to see.

O Lord, Your answers are always good for me.

It's beyond my mind's comprehension that You, my Lord Jesus Christ, answer my prayers.

It's beyond my heart's comprehension that You, my Lord Jesus Christ, answer my prayers.

No Matter How

No matter how loving they are, human beings don't have a heaven to put you and me in.

No matter how good they are, human beings don't have a heaven to put you and me in.

No matter how smart they are, human beings don't have a heaven to put you and me in.

No matter how healthy they are, human beings don't have a heaven to put you and me in.

No matter how trustworthy they are, human beings don't have a heaven to put you and me in.

No matter how rich they are, human beings don't have a heaven to put you and me in.

No matter how educated they are, human beings don't have a heaven to put you and me in.

No matter how skillful they are, human beings don't have a heaven to put you and me in.

No matter how beautiful they are, human beings don't have a heaven to put you and me in.

Only Jesus Christ, the Son of God, has a heaven to put you and me in.

Things Can Go Wrong

Things can go wrong that we have no control over.

We can only hope and pray the Lord will make things right again for us.

Something can go wrong on any day, and we can be so helpless without the Lord helping us to do what we need to do.

Help from the Lord is the best help you and I can ever get day after day.

We can try our best to make things right, but things can still go wrong that we don't' have control over.

We can only hope and pray the Lord will make things right again for us.

It's a miracle when the Lord makes things right again for you and me, who can feel so helpless when things go wrong.

This is the kind of world we live in.

If the Lord doesn't make things right for us, we are helpless.

When You Know

When you know that someone is lying to you, you don't like it when that person wants you to believe that lie.

There is no good reason to tell someone a lie.

Someone may tell you a lie because they are jealous of you.

Someone may tell you a lie because they want to make themselves look good.

There is never a good motive for lying.

If a person lies to you once, then he or she may very well lie to you again.

Someone can tell a lie and believe that it's the truth.

If you love the truth, you will hate lies.

A lie can ruin someone's good name.

If you are a Christian, you won't lie to anyone.

If you are a Christian, you will always tell the truth.

You can't be a Christian and a liar at the same time.

Many liars don't' like to be lied to.

Peter lied to Jesus when he believed that he was telling Jesus the truth.

Peter denied Jesus three times when he didn't believe that he would betray Jesus.

When you know that someone is lying to you, you may not forget that lie for a long time.

Someone who loves to tell lies can never be trusted.

We Need the Lord's Protection

We need the Lord's protection from the devil and his demons.

We can't protect ourselves from evil.

If we have the Lord's protection, we will know it when trouble comes our way.

If we have the Lord's protection, we will know it when sickness comes our way.

If we have the Lord's protection, we will know it when our enemies come our way.

We need the Lord's protection from the devil and his demons every day.

The devil has many human agents, even in the church.

The Lord can protect you and me from those agents.

Many of the devil's human agents go to church while breaking God's commandments.

Many of the devil's human agents hold official positions in the church.

The Pharisees in the bible were religious leaders, but they were really the devil's human agents.

Jesus Christ, our Lord, could always see right through them.

We need the Lord's protection so that we can refuse the devil's human agents.

If we don't pray and choose to love and obey Jesus Christ, we will have no protection at all.

A Dream

A dream is in control of our unconscious mind.

We have no control of where we want to go in a dream.

We have no control of what we want to do in a dream.

We have no control of our choices in a dream.

Whether a dream is good or bad, it can control you and me in our deep sleep.

The Lord can show up in our dreams to protect us.

The Lord can show up in our dreams to comfort us.

People who we've never seen before can show up in our dreams.

Our dreams can carry us from place to place.

A dream has a lot of power over you and me while we are unconscious.

The Lord always knows when to wake us up out of our dreams, whether they're good or bad.

A dream from the Lord is so very refreshing and makes us feel so good when we wake up.

Jesus Will Bring This World to an End

Global warming won't bring this world to an end.

Wars won't bring this world to an end.

Diseases won't bring this world to an end.

Jesus will bring this world to an end like it says in the bible.

Earthquakes won't bring this world to an end.

Crimes won't bring this world to an end.

Droughts won't bring this world to an end.

Jesus will bring this world to an end like it says in the bible.

Hurricanes won't bring this world to an end.

Wildfires won't bring this world to an end.

Floods won't bring this world to an end.

Jesus will bring this world to an end like it says in the bible.

Famines won't bring this world to an end.

Nuclear weapons won't bring this world to an end.

Tornadoes won't bring this world to an end.

Jesus will bring this world to an end when he comes back again like the bible says.

Something Great to Look Forward to

Regardless of all the bad things going on in this world, we have something great to look forward to.

If we are saved, we will go back to heaven with Jesus Christ when he comes back again.

Regardless of all the trials in this world, we have something great to look forward to.

If we are saved in Jesus, we will live forever and ever without sin when Jesus changes us from mortal to immortality.

Regardless of this sinful world coming to an end one day, we have something great to look forward to.

If we are saved in Jesus, we will one day live in a new heaven and new earth.

We have something great to look forward to if we are saved in Jesus Christ, who will give us eternal life one day.

Jesus is looking forward to you and me living with Him in the new Jerusalem Holy City one day.

Even if you and I fall short of god's glory, every day Jesus is looking forward to saving us from our sins to make us children of His kingdom.

We Can Be So Sure

We can be so sure that we are right about something and maybe be so wrong.

It shows that we are not always right about what we are sure of.

Being sure about something doesn't always mean that we are right.

We can be sure about something, and when we see that we're wrong it can shock us.

The only thing that we can always be sure about is Jesus Christ.

We can always be sure that Jesus will save us from our sins if we confess and repent and live our lives doing His will.

We can always be sure that we can put our faith and trust in Jesus every day.

We can always be sure that even if we have a sickness that causes our death, Jesus will give us eternal life when he comes back again to raise us from the grave.

We can be so sure that what we believe must happen.

We can be so sure that what we say must be true.

We can be so sure that what we do must be right.

A fool can be so sure he is wise, until he is in trouble.

There are things that we are sure about, it's true.

We can always be sure that Jesus is our Lord and Savior, who loves us all great and small.

God is a Relationship God

God is a relationship God.

God loves to talk to you and me.

God loves to do good things for you and me.

God loves to comfort you and me.

God loves to help you and me.

God is a relationship God.

God loves to bless you and me.

God loves to lift burdens off of you and me.

God loves to heal you and me.

God is a relationship God.

God loves to protect you and me.

God loves to rescue you and me.

God loves to save you and me from our sins.

God is a relationship God.

I Don't Have it in My Heart

I don't have it in my heart to willfully sin against You, O Lord.

I don't have it in my heart to willfully break Your Commandments, O Lord.

I don't have it in my heart to do my neighbors any evil.

I don't have it in my heart to not love my brothers and sisters in the church.

I don't have it in my heart to not do Your holy will, O Lord.

I don't have it in my heart to tell a lie about anyone.

I don't have it in my heart to not live by Your holy word, O Lord.

I don't have it in my heart to not live by Your holy word, O Lord.

I don't have it in my heart to not help who I can help.

I don't have it in my heart to not pray for loved ones who are not doing Your holy will, O Lord.

I don't have it in my heart to ever turn by back on You, O Lord.

I Am Nothing Without Jesus Christ

I am a window to clean.

I am a forest with no pathway.

I am nothing without Jesus Christ.

I am a bag with holes in it.

I am a chimney full of smoke.

I am nothing without Jesus Christ.

I am a book with dust on it.

I am a rock to pick up and throw.

I am nothing without Jesus Christ.

I am a wall to fall down.

I am a glass to break.

I am nothing without Jesus Christ.

I am a leaf blowing away in the wind.

I am a frame with no picture in it.

I am nothing without Jesus Christ.

I am a light bulb that's blown out.

I am a pen out of ink.

I am nothing without Jesus Christ.

I am a house with nothing in it.

I am a shoe with no laces to tie.

I am nothing without Jesus Christ.

To be Saved

We must believe in Jesus Christ to be saved.

The bible doesn't say that if we are good we will be saved.

The bible doesn't say that if we do good things we will be saved.

There are many good people in this world.

Many good people will risk their lives to save your life and my life.

There are many good people who will let you and me live in their homes.

There are many good people who will feed you and me if we are hungry.

We must believe in Jesus Christ to be saved.

Many people in this world have a heart of gold.

Being good can't give us salvation.

Salvation is in Jesus Christ.

No one can be more good than Jesus Christ.

He is so good to us all every day.

It's a natural thing for us to want good people to make it into heaven.

We must believe in Jesus Christ to be saved and make it into heaven.

Being good is something that Jesus can work with because His goodness leads to repentance.

This Dark and Sinful World

This dark and sinful world loves to shoot us with its bullets of temptation.

This dark and sinful world loves to wound us with its disappointments.

This dark and sinful world loves to beat us up with its grief.

This dark and sinful world loves to knock us out with its troubles.

This dark and sinful world loves to deceive us with its lies.

This dark and sinful world loves to trick us with its failures.

This dark and sinful world loves to charm us with its material things.

Jesus Christ is coming back one day to take you and me out of this dark and sinful world because we are saved in Him.

This dark and sinful world loves to harm us with its greed.

This dark and sinful world loves to captivate us with its attractive views.

One day Jesus will create a new, perfect world with no sin to ever exist again.

Boast About Our Weaknesses

The Apostle Paul had to boast about his weakness so that he could be made strong in the Lord.

He boasted about the terrible things that he went through for Jesus' name sake.

Paul didn't boast that he could speak different languages.

Paul didn't boast about his education.

We need to boast about what Jesus brought us through.

We need to boast about how good Jesus is to us.

We don't need to boast about ourselves, when we're vulnerable to death every day.

When Jesus struck Saul down on the road to Damascus, Saul knew that he couldn't boast about himself anymore.

Jesus gave Saul a new name, Paul, so he could boast about Jesus Christ.

Some church folks boast about their leadership positions in the church.

Some church folks boast about their education and college degrees.

We need to always boast about our weaknesses and uplift and glorify Jesus Christ's holy name.

In Real Life

In real life being married is not always being in love with who you are married to.

In real life falling in love and being in love may be a hundred miles apart.

In real life true love is beyond physical attraction, because physical attraction can fade away.

In real life accepting a rose doesn't mean that love will always last, because feelings can change like the seasons.

In real life we can choose the wrong person to marry, and only time will tell us about the choices we made.

In real life mixed signals can exist in a marriage for years, and it can be stressful if you are having mixed signals.

In real life if Jesus is not in the relationship, it will be unpredictable like the wind blowing in different directions.

Where This World is Heading

The bible tells us that we are heading towards a new heaven and new earth one day.

Every Christian should know this and be happy about that day to come.

We don't need scientists to tell us where this world is heading.

The bible tells us so clear that this world is truly heading to an end of all sin.

Every Christian is heading to heaven through our Lord and Savior Jesus Christ, who has a mansion for us up in heaven.

We can read about where this world is heading in the bible, and no scientist can make that a lie.

Everybody who is saved in Jesus Christ is heading toward eternal life.

Jesus lives in heaven beyond this old sinful world that is heading toward a burning fire and brimstone.

There are All Kinds of Temptations

There are all kinds of temptations in this world.

All temptations are of the devil.

He loves to tempt us to sin against God.

The devil will tempt us every day in some kind of way.

We are all guilty of giving in to his temptations.

The devil's temptations can be so strong that we will give into it if we don't pray and ask Jesus to give us strength.

The devil shows no respect to persons with his temptations.

He can make his temptations look so good in our eyes.

The devil knows our weaknesses and tempts us where we are weak.

He loves to catch us off guard with his temptations.

Even though the devil loves to tempt us, God has given us free will to choose to not sin against Him.

Jesus has given us the power to resist the devil's temptations.

Jesus was tempted by the devil in the wilderness for forty days and forty nights.

Jesus did not give in to the devil's temptations because He always prayed to His heavenly Father.

Jesus spoke the word of God to the devil and made him flee.

There are all kinds of temptations in this world.

Jesus overcame them all for us by shedding His blood on the cross for our sins.

A New World Began

A new world began with Noah and his family.

This new world that we are living in is not without sin.

Noah's son proved that when he looked at his father's nakedness and made fun of him.

The old world passed away in the worldwide flood that destroyed everyone except Noah and his family.

Another new world will begin when all the saints come down from heaven after a thousand years.

Jesus Christ will destroy this world with fire and brimstone that will rain down on all the fallen angels and all the wicked people.

Another new world will begin without sin one day.

All the righteous will live in the new world with Jesus Christ, who will bring the new Jerusalem Holy City to this world after a thousand years in heaven.

A new world began with Noah and his family.

The old world was filled with sin everywhere, and this new world is filled with sin everywhere.

This new world will be destroyed like the old world, and another new world will be created thanks to Jesus Christ, our Lord and Savior.

In Our Hearts

Many people can write a novel.

They can't write it in people's hearts.

Many people can write a journal.

They can't write it in people's hearts.

Many people can write a note.

They can't write it in people's hearts.

Many people can write a fiction book.

They can't write it in people's hearts.

Many people can write a non-fiction book.

They can't write it in people's hearts.

Only Jesus Christ has written His law in our hearts.

Children will feel guilty for being punished if they disobey their parents.

We will feel guilty for being caught in a lie.

We will feel guilty for stealing something and getting caught.

Only Jesus Christ has written his laws in our hearts.

We will feel guilty for killing someone and being caught.

We will feel guilty for saying something wrong and being caught.

Only Jesus Christ has written his laws in our hearts.

The Lord Predestined Us

The Lord predestined us to be born at the right time for us to live in this world.

Everybody in this world was born at the right time.

Hundreds of years ago wasn't the right time for you and me to exist.

Thousands of years ago wasn't the right time for you and me to be born and live in this world.

The Lord always knows what is good for us and right for us.

If the Lord wanted you and me to be born a thousand years ago, He would've made that happen.

The Lord knows that hundreds or thousands of years ago we weren't meant to be here.

The Lord knows that this present time is our time to live and to do His holy will.

If you and I were born hundreds or thousands of years ago, we may not have been so conscious of the choices that we make.

We are pretty much aware of our choices today.

No one was ever born at the wrong time.

The Lord predestined us to all live in this present day.

Being Selfish

Being selfish can cause people to be murderers.

Being selfish can cause people to be child molesters.

Being selfish can cause people to be abusive.

Being selfish can cause people to be rapists.

Being selfish can cause people to be proud.

Being selfish can cause people to be controlling.

Being selfish can cause people to be thieves.

Being selfish can cause people to be greedy.

Being selfish can cause people to be mean.

Being selfish can cause people to be terrorists.

Being selfish is of the devil, who is selfish all the time.

Only Jesus Christ was selfless all the time when He lived on earth among many selfish people.

Just Because We Are Christians

Just because we are Christians doesn't mean we have no flaws.

Just because we are Christians doesn't mean we won't make any mistakes.

Just because we are Christians doesn't mean we will always say the right words.

Just because we are Christians doesn't mean we will always do the right deeds.

Just because we are Christians doesn't mean everything will be good for us all the time.

Just because we are Christians doesn't mean we are perfect and without sin.

Abraham was a Christian, but he made some mistakes.

Jacob was a Christian, but he made some mistakes.

Moses was a Christian, but he made some mistakes.

Everybody in the bible made some mistakes, except Jesus Christ, who was the only one without sin.

Just because we are Christians doesn't mean we will eat right all the time.

Just because we are Christians doesn't mean we will think right all the time.

Just because we are Christians doesn't mean we will always have the right motives.

Being cleansed in the blood of Jesus is a lifetime cleansing for all Christians.

O Lord, I Need You so Much

O Lord, I need You so much in my thoughts.

O Lord, I need You so much in what I say.

O Lord, I need You so much in my motives.

O Lord, I need You so much in my intentions.

O Lord, I need You so much in my mind.

O Lord, I need You so much in my dreams.

O Lord, I need You so much in my house.

O Lord, I need You so much in my marriage.

O Lord, I need You so much on the road.

O Lord, I need You so much on my good days.

O Lord, I need You so much on my bad days.

O Lord, I need You so much in my trials.

O Lord, I need You so much in the church.

O Lord, I need You so much wherever I go.

O Lord, I need You so much in my life.

O Lord, I need You so much in my heart.

O Lord, I need You so much in the choices I make day after day.

O Lord, I need You so much in my destiny.

In the Bad Weather of Life

Some people believe that they can drive fast in bad weather.

Some people believe that they can go surfing in bad weather.

Some people believe that they can go fishing in bad weather.

Some people believe that they party in bad weather.

Some people believe that they can do anything in bad weather.

In the bad weather of life, many people believe they can disobey the Lord and not reap the consequences.

Some people believe that they can play in bad weather.

Some people believe that they can camp out in bad weather.

Some people believe that they can go jogging in bad weather.

In the bad weather of life, many people believe they can pray to the Lord while living in their sins.

Some people believe that they can go anywhere in bad weather.

Some people believe that nothing bad will happen to them in bad weather.

Some people believe that they can ride out the bad weather when they are told to leave the area.

In the bad weather of life, many people believe that they can turn their backs on the Lord and feel safe to walk into the unknown.

The Devil's Work

Sicknesses are the devil's work.

Diseases are the devil's work.

Crimes are the devil's work.

Wars are the devil's work.

Heat waves are the devil's work.

Forest fires are the devil's work.

Droughts are the devil's work.

Floods are the devil's work.

Tornadoes are the devil's work.

Hurricanes are the devil's work.

The devil loves to deceive whoever he can to make them believe that God makes bad things happen.

The devil loves for people to blame God for his evil works.

In the bible it was the devil who caused the strong winds to blow Job's children's house down, which killed all of his children.

It was the devil who caused sores to break out all over Job's body.

The devil wanted to take Job's life, but God didn't let the devil win.

Don't blame God for the devil's work.

After This Life is Over

After this life is over, there are no more chances to love Jesus Christ with all your mind, heart, strength and soul.

After this life is over, there are no more chances to love thy neighbor as you love thyself.

After this life is over, there are no more chances to not use the Lord's name in vain.

After this life is over, there are no more chances to remember to keep the Sabbath day holy.

After this life is over, there are no more chances to not kill.

After this life is over, there are no more chances to not steal.

After this life is over, there are no more chances to not bear false witness against thy neighbor.

After this life is over, there are no more chances to obey your parents.

After this life is over, there are no more chances to keep God's commandments.

After this life is over, it will be too late to keep God's commandments.

His commandments are freedom, love, perfection, righteousness, holy and good to all great and small.

After this life is over, there are no more chances to make Jesus Christ our choice.

After this life is over, there are no more chances to be saved in Jesus.

It's Easy to Sin Against God

It's easy to sin against God, because we live in a sinful world.

It's easy to say something bad.

It's easy to do something bad.

It's easy to feel proud about what we say.

It's easy to feel proud about what we know.

It's easy to feel proud about what we do.

It's easy to sin against God, because we live in a sinful world.

It's easy to make a mistake.

It's easy to have a bad habit.

It's easy to think on bad things.

It's easy to have bad motives.

It's easy to have bad intentions.

It's easy to sin against God, because we live in a sinful world.

Jesus Christ died for our sins and He rose from the grave to give us the victory over our sins.

No matter how easy it is to sin against God, Jesus can give us the strength to resist the devil's sinful temptations if we pray to Him for strength.

Our free will choices are easy to use to serve the Lord or to serve the devil.

Fighting in a War of Sin

I dreamed that I was in a squad unit of soldiers.

We were out in the woods and fighting against the enemy soldiers.

Then the scene changed to another squad of soldiers that I was in, and we were preparing to fight the enemy.

One of the soldiers in the squad said to the other soldiers, "Don't shoot at them because they are friendly soldiers."

Then a group of solders had come behind my squad and could've shot us and killed us all, but it turned out that they were the friendly soldiers that had disappeared in the scene.

My squad and I were happy that they were friendly soldiers who had come up behind us so unexpectedly.

We then knew that wherever we were in the dense woods, we were not alone when fighting the enemy soldiers.

We knew that the friendly soldiers who were not in our squad would be nearby to help us fight the war.

Our Lord and Savior Jesus Christ is our best friend who will always be near to us to help us fight in the war against sin.

As long as we keep our trust in Him, we can know that He will cover our backs against that old devil who would love to kill us dead.

We can fight and win the war with Jesus, who has overcome all of our sins.

Blessed with Enough

O Lord, You blessed me with enough mental health to survive from day to day.

O Lord, You blessed me with enough physical health to survive from day to day.

O Lord, You blessed me with enough education to survive from day to day.

O Lord, You blessed me with enough common sense to survive from day to day.

O Lord, You blessed me with enough faith in You for me to spiritually survive from day to day.

O Lord, You blessed me with enough hope in You for me to spiritually survive from day to day.

O Lord, You blessed me with enough love for You for me to spiritually survive from day to day.

O Lord, You blessed me with enough of Your blessings for me to survive from day to day.

We Church Folks

We church folks need to know how to be real with people.

We church folks have real problems in our lives.

We don't need to act like we are so holy and righteous and don't have any problems.

We church folks need to come down off our spiritual high and meet people where they are in their real problems.

Jesus met people where they were, even though He was worthy to always be on a spiritual high.

We church folks are not without sin.

We have some real sinful problems, just like all people of the world.

Jesus Christ was very real with people all the time.

Jesus was always real with love in His heart for everyone, even though not everyone loved Him.

We church folks need to always be real with one another.

Loving people and being real means not controlling people and trying to make them do what we want.

Nothing in this world is more real than love.

Without love, we would be so phony all the time.

We church folks need Jesus to help us to be real about what we say and do every day.

Your Feelings Can Get Hurt

No matter how beautiful you are, your feelings can get hurt.

No matter how strong you are, your feelings can get hurt.

No matter how smart you are, your feelings can get hurt.

No matter how educated you are, your feelings can get hurt.

No matter how skillful you are, your feelings can get hurt.

No matter how brave you are, your feelings can get hurt.

No matter how good you are, your feelings can get hurt.

No matter how bad you are, your feelings can get hurt.

No matter how gifted you are, your feelings can get hurt.

No matter how talented you are, your feelings can get hurt.

No matter how tough you are, your feelings can get hurt.

No matter how rich you are, your feelings can get hurt.

When Peter denied Jesus Christ three times, Peter must have hurt Jesus' feelings.

Only a fool would deny that our feelings can't be hurt by many things.

Jesus gave us feelings so we would know we are human.

When the Lord Wakes Me Up

When the Lord wakes me up in the morning, I am not blind. I can see the daylight all around me.

When the Lord wakes me up in the morning, I am not deaf. I can hear the traffic on the road and I can hear my neighbors talking.

When the Lord wakes me up in the morning, I am not paralyzed. I can get up out of my bed and stand up with my feet on the floor.

When the Lord wakes me up in the morning, I need no oxygen tank to help me breathe. I can breathe on my own.

When the Lord wakes me up in the morning, I am not insane. I am sane in my mind.

When the Lord wakes me up in the morning, I am so blessed to be alive and in good health.

When the Lord wakes you and me up in the morning, we should think Him before we even get out of our beds.

Life, health, and strength all come from the Lord.

We cannot buy or sell these things.

No one can tell me that the Lord is not good to me.

God Is

God is on top of the mountains.

God is down in the valleys.

God is under the oceans.

God is out in the universe.

God is in the caves.

God is in the bible.

God is in very race, creed and culture of people.

God is in nature.

God is in our hearts.

God is in heaven.

God is everywhere, because everywhere belongs to God.

A Storm Can Frighten Us

One day in the late afternoon, a storm appeared.

There was thunder and lightning, and rain and hail were falling from the sky.

I was in my house with my two little dogs.

My dogs were afraid of the storm.

One of my dogs laid down under the chair I wanted to sit in.

I sat down in the chair and very quietly watched the storm as I prayed to the Lord for His protection.

The Lord surely did protect me and my dogs from the storm and its strong winds blowing so fierce.

I was afraid of the storm.

I didn't want the lightning to strike me or my dogs.

The Lord will often use a spiritual storm to frighten us in order to help us to wise up.

That spiritual storm may be a sickness or the loss of a loved one, but it's meant to make us put our trust in Him.

The spiritual storms have their thunder and lightning that let us know we need Jesus Christ, the Lord, in our lives.

A storm can frighten us because it's so much bigger than us.

The storm is not bigger than the Lord, who the storms will obey.

A Smile Can Lift People Up

One morning, I left the house and went to the store.

When I got there, I shopped for some food to eat.

After I was through with shopping, I went up to the checkout line.

A man was in front of me waiting to check out.

As I was standing there in line, the cashier looked at me and said, "You are always smiling when I see you. Why aren't you smiling today? Are you deep in thought?"

I said I was and she said, "Sometimes I'll be deep in thought and not smiling too."

I told her that it's always good to smile.

She agreed and said, "A smile can cause people to smile back at you."

We both agreed with that statement, and I realized there was a lesson here.

When we smile at people, it can lift them up.

A smile is a gift from the Lord.

I believe that Jesus Christ, my Lord and Savior, smiled a lot to lift people up beyond healing them of their sicknesses.

When Jesus smiled at people, it must have been the truest smile they had ever seen.

Mr. Selfishness and Mr. Humility

Mr. Selfishness and Mr. Humility are members of the church body.

They go to church to worship the Lord Jesus Christ.

At the church service, they both had to take communion.

Mr. Selfishness said to Mr. Humility, "I will not get down on my knees to wash your feet."

Mr. Selfishness just didn't care about getting rid of his pride.

Mr. Selfishness took off his shoes and socks to get his feet washed.

Mr. Humility said to Mr. Selfishness, "If you love Jesus, you would want to be like Jesus. Jesus humbled Himself and got down on His knees to wash His disciples' feet.

Jesus showed his disciples that they must get rid of their pride to be like Him."

Mr. Humility said to Mr. Selfishness, "You can go to church all of your life, but if you don't humble yourself before the Lord your worship is in vain."

Mr. Selfishness said to Mr. Humility, "I just can't stoop down that low to wash your feet. I am too high up in society to get down on my knees to do that."

Mr. Humility said to Mr. Selfishness, "Jesus Christ, my Lord and Savior, does not know you even though you go to church.

Jesus has no part of you because you are not in His communion of self-denial."

Civilized

Being civilized is to use your good common sense.

Being civilized is to be educated.

Being civilized is to treat everybody right.

There are people who believe they are the most civilized people on earth.

They want to be superior people and think they are above other people they believe aren't civilized.

What is so civilized about killing people because they look different?

What is so civilized about oppressing people because they look different?

Being civilized is having good morals.

Being civilized is loving everybody the same.

Jesus Christ, the Lord, was the most civilized human being on earth.

Jesus didn't live His life as though He was superior to others.

Jesus was the humblest human being who ever lived on earth.

Even though Jesus was superior, He didn't act like He was better than other people.

Only Jesus Christ deserves to be superior over angels and men.

His love for us is superb, above all civilization.

Speak the Truth in Love

We Christians must always speak the truth to people in love.

We aren't supposed to speak the truth to people like we want to boss them around with it.

We Christians must always speak the truth to people in love.

We aren't supposed to speak the truth in anger or try to make people live by the truth of God's holy word.

The truth is love.

The truth is not to control anyone and make them live by the truth.

The truth is not anger to make people feel afraid of the truth.

We Christians must always speak the truth to people in love.

We aren't supposed to speak the truth to try to make people feel bad.

We aren't supposed to speak the truth to try to make people feel guilty.

Speaking the truth to people in love can soften their hearts and cause them to want to live by the truth.

The truth can harden people's hearts if it is not spoken in love.

Jesus Christ, our Lord and Savior, always spoke the truth in love even to his enemies and he died for them to save them from their sins.

Worth Putting Above

Is a human being worth putting above the Lord?

Is a job worth putting above the Lord?

Is a business worth putting above the Lord?

Is a house worth putting above the Lord?

Is a car worth putting above the Lord?

Is a truck worth putting above the Lord?

Is a anything worth putting above the Lord?

Many people have put someone above the Lord.

Many people have put things above the Lord.

They left the church to be with someone.

They left the church for a job.

They left the church for a career.

They left the church for a business.

They left the church for a car.

They left the church for a truck.

They left the church for whatever they believed to be better than the Lord.

Miraculous

O Lord, Your love is miraculous.

O Lord, Your mercy is miraculous.

O Lord, Your grace is miraculous.

O Lord, Your truth is miraculous.

O Lord, Your goodness is miraculous.

O Lord, Your protection is miraculous.

O Lord, Your forgiveness is miraculous.

O Lord, Your long suffering is miraculous.

O Lord, Your healing is miraculous.

O Lord, Your spiritual gifts are miraculous.

O Lord, You giving me life, health and strength is miraculous.

O Lord, You are miraculous!

The Power of the Holy Ghost

I dreamed about a man I had prayed for. I dreamed that I was in a building filled with people I didn't know.

We were all sitting down and talking.

Then, all of a sudden, this one man that I knew asked me if I would pray for him because he had cancer.

He walked over to my table and I stood up and took off my hat, then I began to pray for him.

As I was praying, I was a little fearful of the crowd of people.

I continued to pray despite the fear, and the man and the crowd started praying along with me.

Then, the power of the Holy Ghost filled the place as I laid my hand on the man's head while I kept praying for him.

My prayer got louder and louder as did the prayers from the crowd.

I felt the power of the Holy Ghost moving all over the place.

As I continued to pray, some church members walked into the building.

They were surprised to see me praying in front of a large crowd of people.

The Lord was with me, the ill man and the people in the crowd who loved the Lord Jesus Christ with the power of His Holy Ghost.

If It Were Possible

If it were possible that there would be a cure for cancer.

If it were possible that there would be a vaccine for the corona virus.

If it were possible that no new disease will break out.

God has nothing to do with it all.

We, the people in this world, bring these sicknesses upon ourselves.

We are not always cautious of what we eat and what we drink.

We are not always cautious of having good hygiene by always washing our hands and covering up our mouths when we cough.

If it were possible that there would be no more crimes, no more wars and no more bloodshed.

If it were possible that everybody would love one another.

Jesus Christ had prayed that if it were possible that the awful hour awaiting him might pass him by.

He cried out to His heavenly Father and said, "Everything is possible for you."

There is nothing impossible with God, but we do reap what we sow.

God's Reasons

Man doesn't know God's reasons for allowing bad things to happen all around the world.

You and I don't know why God allows many people to get cancer.

God doesn't have to reveal His reasons to us.

We don't know why God allows many diseases and viruses to break out.

We don't know why God allows many babies to be born with birth defects.

God's reasons are not for us to always know.

If God reveals some of His reasons to us, we might be shocked and say what a fool we are to question God's reasons.

God's reasons are always right.

Our reasons are not always right.

No matter how many bad things are going on in this world, we can always trust God's reasons to be right beyond the bad things.

Being a Christian

Being a Christian is having faith in Jesus Christ.

Being a Christian is loving and obeying Jesus Christ.

Either you and I are Christians or we are not Christians.

We can't have one foot in the church and one foot out of the church.

Being a Christian is nothing to play around with.

Being a Christian is nothing to take lightly.

A Christian can't live in the light and live in the darkness too.

Being a Christian is a very serious walk with the Lord Jesus Christ.

Being a Christian is that we must do what we say about the Lord.

Being a Christian is no fairy tale life to live.

Being a Christian is no delusional life to live.

Being a Christian is real life because Jesus Christ is real.

We can't live in sin and be a Christian.

We must confess and repent of our sins to be a Christian.

The Truth

Many people don't like to hear the truth.

Many people won't accept the truth.

Many people will run away from the truth.

Many people won't tell the truth.

Many people won't like you and me for telling the truth.

Many people don't like the truth stepping on their toes.

A few people will always tell the truth.

Many people don't live by the truth of God's holy word.

Many people don't want to hear the truth of God's holy word.

Many people will cover up the truth.

The truth is freedom.

The truth is real.

The truth is the Lord and Savior Jesus Christ.

The truth is everlasting.

The truth is in the bible.

The truth is God.

The truth is the Holy Spirit.

There is a True Living God

There is a true living God who answers the prayers of His children.

God loves everybody, but especially His obedient children who love Him in return.

God doesn't answer the prayers of the wicked who rebel against Him.

God will surely make good things happen to anyone who believes in his Son, Jesus Christ.

God also allows good things to happen to many wicked people who are not too wicked for God to also bless.

There is a true living God who knows the beginning of our lives to the end of our lives.

God is not too hard on the wicked and won't deny them a chance to confess and repent of their sins.

There is a true living God who won't put onto us more than what we can bear.

God knows that He can help us to bear even death.

We wouldn't know anything and couldn't feel suffering and pain in death.

There is a true living God who won't allow this world to self-destruct.

God will save all of His children until the end of this world that He will destroy.

Dealing with Self

Dealing with self can be hard to do.

Dealing with self can be a challenge.

Dealing with self can be some ups and downs.

Dealing with self can be a hard road to walk down.

Dealing with self can sometimes be harder than dealing with someone else.

You and I need Jesus to help us deal with self.

Jesus Christ had to deal with self.

He had to pray to His heavenly Father to give Him the strength to drink the cup of wrath for our sins.

Jesus said to His heavenly Father, "It's not my will but Your will."

Dealing with self is a mountain to climb and a valley to walk down in day after day.

Dealing with self is being aware of yourself who is a sinner needing Jesus Christ, who deals with sinners to save.

When the Lord Tells Us

When the Lord tells us to do something, we need to do it.

The Lord will always tell us to do something that is good and right for us.

The Lord won't tell us to do something that He knows we can't do.

He knows that some people will be blessed by what we do when the Lord tells us to do it.

When the Lord tells us to do something, we must not hesitate to do it.

We will be uplifted when we do what the Lord tells us to do.

We will be blessed when we do what the Lord tells us to do.

The Lord will never tell us to do something bad.

The Lord will always tell us to do something that will help others.

The Lord will always tell us to do something that will last a long time.

When the Lord tells us to do something, we will never regret it.

We will sooner or later regret not doing what the Lord tells us to do.

Life is Short

Life is short.

We should try our best to enjoy as much of it as we can.

If the Lord blesses us to have some good things in our lives, then we should enjoy them and give the praise and glory to God.

If the Lord blesses us with good mental and physical health, we should enjoy it and use our minds and bodies to do the Lord's will.

Life is short.

If the Lord blesses us financially and we are able to live good prosperous lives, then we should enjoy it and thank the Lord for blessing us financially.

Life is short.

We have a free will choice to live our lives unto the Lord every day.

Life is short.

The bad choices we make can surely make our lives so much shorter.

Life is short.

We should enjoy life, regardless of the trials we go through because they draw us closer to the Lord.

Just Because You Are

Just because you are gifted, it doesn't mean that you don't need to improve.

Just because you are talented, it doesn't mean that you won't have any problems.

Just because you are brilliant, it doesn't mean that you won't make any mistakes.

Just because you are good, it doesn't mean that you won't do something wrong.

Just because you are smart, it doesn't mean that you won't do something stupid.

With all the wisdom that King Salomon had, he still made some foolish choices that God was not pleased with.

Only Jesus Christ was without sin to be perfect in words and deeds.

Until Our Love is Tested

We don't know what love is until our love is tested.

Love is truly tested through the hard times that will tell the truth about love.

As long as life is good, it's easy to love your spouse and your children.

As long as life is going good for any Christian, it's easy to love the Lord.

Our love will be tested sooner or later.

The Lord will test our love for Him to show if we truly love Him or don't love Him.

The hard times in life can surely strengthen our love or weaken our love to get cold like ice.

Until our love is tested, we don't know what love is.

Only God truly knows what love is because God is love.

You and I are not love.

Our love can fail through the hard times when things are going bad in our lives.

Most of the Time

Most of the time what we say is what we are made of.

Most of the time what we do is what we are made of.

Sometimes, what we say is not what we meant to say.

Most of the time we are aware of what we do.

People who are in their right frame of mind pretty much know what they do.

Because of being born in sin, we are not always aware of what we do that can be questioned.

Only Jesus Christ was without sin to always be aware of what He said and what He did when He lived on earth.

As Light as a Feather

If we give our burdens to the Lord, He can make our burdens as light as a feather on any given day.

The Lord is the greatest burden lifter for us, make no mistake in any kind of weather.

The Lord can make our burdens fly as free as a bird that has feathers that we can see whether we live in the north, south, east or west.

As light as a feather our burdens will be lifted for giving them to Jesus Christ, our Lord, who loves you and me.

I can't lift your burdens and you can't lift my burdens better than Jesus who we should not question.

He can make our burdens as light as a feather to drift away like a boat that has no one in it.

Not a Place to Go To

The church is not a place to go to just to look good.

That doesn't mean a thing to the Lord if our hearts are hard as wood.

The church is not a place to go to just to socialize.

That doesn't mean a thing to the Lord if we don't have a relationship with Him who is all wise when we talk to Him, who is in heaven on high.

The church is not a place to go to just because it's tradition.

That doesn't mean a thing to the Lord who wants to transition our lives to put us in a position to be saved in Him.

The church is a place to go to and be the church bride of Jesus Christ.

Every day we can always confide in Jesus with all of our hearts that Jesus won't deny.

There is Not a Day That Goes By

There is not a day that goes by, O Lord, that I don't need Your love.

There is not a day that goes by, O Lord, that I don't need Your protection that is miraculous in my eyes.

There is not a day that goes by, O Lord, that I don't need Your mercy upon my soul that cries out unto You who cannot lie to me on each day that goes by.

There is not a day that goes by that I don't need Your grace, O Lord, that You save me in for me to face up to the day.

There Are People in this World

There are people in this world that you just don't like, but you must love their soul to be saved in Jesus Christ.

Jesus didn't like the pharisees, but he loved their souls to be saved in Him.

There are people in this world who you just don't like to be around, but you must love their souls to be saved in Jesus Christ.

Jesus didn't like being around the hypocritical Pharisees day after day.

There are people in this world who you just don't trust, but you must love their souls to be saved in Jesus Christ.

Jesus didn't trust the Pharisees who were out to kill him.

There are church folks who you just don't trust, but you must love their souls to be saved in Jesus Christ.

Everybody in the church doesn't mean you good and well.

If you are a true Christian, you will love everybody even though you won't like everybody's ways.

Jesus didn't like everybody's ways when He lived on earth.

Comfortable

The devil wants people to be comfortable living in their sins so that he can cause their souls to be lost.

We should never be comfortable about sinning against God.

If you and I are comfortable, then we are in danger of God's judgment upon us.

The devil doesn't want us to be serious about doing God's holy will.

The devil doesn't want us to be serious about denying ourselves and picking up our crosses to follow Jesus Christ.

Being comfortable living in sin is being a friend to the devil.

Being comfortable living in sin is like being married to the devil.

If we hate sin, we are a friend to the Lord.

Any born-again believer in Jesus Christ will never become comfortable about sinning against God.

Being comfortable living in sin is the devil's pride and joy.

We Don't Have to Explain

We don't have to explain anything to the Lord.

He already knows our situations.

He sees them before we see them coming our way.

The Lord doesn't have to explain anything to you and me; we are not all-knowing.

You and I will often have to explain things to one another.

We don't understand everything.

The Lord Jesus Christ understands everything.

We are so blessed that we don't have to explain anything to the Lord.

We can try to explain something to one another when we don't understand what's being said.

Trying to explain something to a little child can be hard to do at times.

Many adults don't have good understanding about some things.

We don't have to explain any of our problems to the Lord, who can solve them all.

We must know what we are talking about to explain things to one another.

The Lord has to come down on our level to explain things to us.

The Lord has to explain some things to the most brilliant and most educated people in this world.

When the Lord explains things to us, He will always make sure that we understand Him who can make His holy word to be so clear to us.

We Don't Have to Explain

We don't have to explain anything to the Lord.

He already knows our situations.

He sees them before we see them coming our way.

The Lord doesn't have to explain anything to you and me who are not all-knowing.

You and I will often have to explain things to one another.

We don't understand everything.

The Lord Jesus Christ understands everything.

We are so blessed that we don't have to explain anything to the Lord.

We can try to explain something to one another who may not understand what is being said.

Trying to explain something to someone is not always easy to do.

Trying to especially explain something to a little child can be hard to do at times.

Many adults don't have good understanding about some things.

We don't have to explain any of our problems to the Lord who can solve them all.

We must know what we are talking about to explain things to one another.

The Lord has to come down on our level to explain things to us.

The Lord has to explain some things to the most brlliant and most eduated people in this world.

When the Lord explains things to us, He will always make sure that we understand Him who can make His holy word to be so clear to us.

www.ingramcontent.com/pod-product-compliance
Lightning Source LLC
Chambersburg PA
CBHW072036110526
44592CB00012B/1444